P9-CCE-463

Wildflowers in Your House

JOSEPHINE VON MIKLOS

Wildflowers in Your House

WITH 227 BLACK-AND-WHITE

AND 8 FULL COLOR PHOTOGRAPHS

BY THE AUTHOR

AND 108 BOUQUETS

MOSTLY BY ANNE H. STRAUS

1968

DOUBLEDAY & COMPANY, INC., GARDEN CITY, NEW YORK

This book belongs to all who with love, enthusiasm, good humor, and angelic patience slaved to help me do it: my sister Barbara Bogdan, my friends Helen Federico, Kappi Getsinger, Ricky Goldfinger, Mary Halle, Roger S. Halle, Vlasta Halle, Elizabeth Haas, Harold Jackson, Marjorie Maas, Abby Merriam, William Pahlmann, Margery Sachs, Bill Straus, Wendy Straus, and Roslyn Wood.

LIBRARY OF CONGRESS CATALOG CARD NUMBER 68–18101
COPYRIGHT © 1968 BY JOSEPHINE VON MIKLOS
ALL RIGHTS RESERVED
PRINTED IN THE UNITED STATES OF AMERICA
FIRST EDITION

Contents

Preface

Wild plants and flowers are with us almost all year around: in spring, summer, and autumn when they dot the countryside in thousandfold abundance, and in the winter when nuts and berries and evergreens continue to live throughout the season.

Wild plants and flowers grow everywhere: in the fields and meadows, along the roads we drive or walk on; flanking railroad tracks or embroidering old and otherwise abandoned places of waste. They are in and around ponds and streams and rivers, and in the woods, often hidden behind the trees or boulders or under the mulch of leaves, but they are there.

Wild plants and flowers are *free*. There is no price tag on them, no commercial law of supply and demand. They are the wonderful and extravagant *gifts* which nature showers upon us . . . ours for the picking and bundling and bringing home to give us pleasure for many days if only we treat them gently and with a little tenderness. Many of them can even be transplanted into our own gardens so that we may enjoy them close at hand.

Everywhere in our houses or city apartments and for every ordinary day or festive occasion there is a place for them. Many of the flowers mix well with one another and with grasses and leaves. They give us happy patches of color to make our mood brighter, our daily tasks easier, and give pleasure to our family and friends. They make lovely little shapes on a breakfast tray or desk; or grandiose plumes of vibrating beauty on our piano or formal dinner table. They may be simple in design or subtle, or lusty and strong. But they will fit everywhere and with almost everything.

No matter what style or period your house: a Victorian mansion, an old farmhouse, a Cape Cod cottage, a suburban "split level" or an ultracontemporary dream of glass and steel, a chic penthouse on Fifth Avenue or a small apartment in a walk-up, an A-frame on a mountaintop or a weekend cabin which you and your son have built, wild plants and flowers will be right and fitting.

We have carefully and quite on purpose avoided the term "arrangement" in this book. While no one denies that "flower arrangements" using cultivated plants done with care and often great artistry can be very beautiful, they are always made according to a precise plan, the dictates of a definite style, and following specific directions.

The "bouquets" in this book were made with no such restrictions. They were put together with whatever plants were in season and easily found. The people who made them derived great pleasure in going out and gathering an armful of flowers and leaves and grasses and putting them in whatever container was at hand or seemed right for the time and place.

One can float a single blossom in a shallow plate; use a nicely shaped bottle or jar from the Supermarket which used to hold vinegar or jam or a can from which only yesterday one served tomato soup; a piece of glassware from a son's chemistry set, or a precious old piece of hand-cut crystal treasured in one's family for generations; whatever one has at hand, whatever one uses will be right and fitting if it pleases *us* . . . and if the plants seem happy in it.

This book is intended as a *guide*, and the bouquets in it are merely samples of what anyone can do all over the house. Perhaps none of them is exactly what *you* will do once you start to think of wildflowers as decorations. Go on from here. Also, not every wild plant grows in every location, nor will you own the same or even similar containers we have used. But almost everyone has collected things over the years whether they are precious or just practical everyday things.

Almost every bouquet is accompanied by photographs of the plants used; in some instances there are two photographs if the design of the flower was especially beautiful and amazing. But then, all of them are. In a few instances we have used a second picture of the same plant if it seemed to make things simpler.

The color photographs beginning on page 65 were designed with the same purpose but a somewhat different approach. We do not say, "Put this or that bouquet on this or that kind of table," as we do with those in black and white. All we mean is to show the marvelous colors of some of the flowers in combination with others and seen from a historical point of view. The periods chosen were favorites and can, of course, be changed at will as long as you observe the basic feeling of the times you wish to portray. Can't you imagine the fun we had when we tried to find flowers which would match a period? Or when we found the Mallow which matched an ancestor's wedding dress?

There is a marvelous thing about wildflowers: they fall into place by themselves.

All of us in making the bouquets had *fun*. They gave us a lift. They served us well wherever we used them. We hope you will find the same delight in making *your* bouquets.

We know no happier way to share the riches which the Creator's hand has strewn upon the blooming earth.

JOSEPHINE VON MIKLOS

Pound Ridge, N.Y., August 1967

Introduction to Color

The *color* of a wildflower, the *surroundings* in which you find it and the *light* in which you see it are the three most important factors when you decide to use it in a room.

Everyone is more sensitive to color than they realize and nowhere is this more true than with the color of wildflowers. We see them first against the color of their natural habitat . . . the greens and browns of mosses, the grays of rock and sand, the blue of the sky, the changing whites of the clouds . . . which make us feel that the flower, regardless of its own color, is a special experience. The first glimpse of the flower is a direct communication to the emotions, bringing a sense of affirmation, of wonder, and of hope; you feel that a wildflower is not a *reflection* of beauty but its full reality.

Something of the experience of finding a wildflower should be mirrored in the way you use it in your house. Any bouquet of wildflowers is or should be a conversation piece, no matter how modest. For the chalk-white of Star-of-Bethlehem in a low black bowl on a contemporary granite coffee table should be just as breath-taking as a great big mass of Lilies with Daisies and grasses, Black-eyed Susans and Blue Vetch, in the center of a polished antique dining room table.

Some flowers are flamboyant no matter where they are—Goldenrod, Mullein, Meadow Lilies, Giant Purple Loosestrife, and Joe-Pye-Weed suggest large and flamboyant bouquets in large rooms—but for the most part wildflowers are shy, small in scale, delicate in line, provocative in color, intimate, friendly and unobtrusive and can be used in the smallest corners. Violets with their wide range of color, from white to pink and yellow to deep purple are friendly. Buttercups, Daisies, Black-eyed Susans, Bouncing Bet, Vervain, are extrovert, sturdy, universally loved. All of them are as decorative in a room as they are fun to find beside a road, along a fence, or on a railroad embankment.

But when one picks a wildflower it is not for its color alone or to compliment the color scheme of a room. Much of its interest lies in its form, the quality of its line, or even in its place in cultural history.

The choice of a container for a wildflower may seem casual but it should be a thoughtful and considered act. Remember the color and texture of the original habitat of the plant and try to recapture some of this feeling with both the container and the place in your house in which you use it. You may remember the brilliance of yellow Mustard beside the road and discover that after you have put it into a deep ruby jug and then placed it in your library, the sun will make the colors sing, along with those of the books behind the Mustard and the jug. Or if you place on the window sill of your bedroom where you look first thing in the morning when you wake up to see what the weather is like, an amusing bottle with delicate Beardtongue and sweet Bluebells, even the foggy outside will look more cheerful. Surely a few branches of Shadbush in bloom in a white apothecary jar will brighten the darkest corner.

There are other pleasures which come to us when we add a living flower or bouquet to a room: a feeling of pride when we are knowledgeable enough to choose the best possible color to bring an accent to the color scheme of a room; the delight when you have, perhaps, grown the wildflower in your own garden—as more and more people are doing today—and it enhances every part of your living room. But the greatest joy of all is to find a wildflower which you did not know before in the woods or nearby meadow, or even along the sides of the road and can now learn all about it and fit it with other plants into the daily, living design of your house.

Exactly, then, from a color point of view, where does your thinking change when you wish to use wildflowers rather than garden flowers in your rooms?

If you have a glorious perennial or cutting garden to choose from or the lighted window of a florist shop to ponder a long time before you decide on pink rather than red carnations, you would be quite right not to rush your decision. But with wildflowers color tells a pure story and includes the relationship between twig, leaf, and flower and the consideration of the color and form of every part. Each wildflower brings with it its own excitement and therefore it usually happens that the color scheme of the bouquet for a breakfast tray for the guest room is planned *around the flower*. There is real excitement in picking a large Mullein plant and putting it into a jar to enhance the brown siding of a contemporary house or making an enormous bouquet of Bittersweet for a large Chinese vase on your grand piano.

In another way all those beautiful wildflowers which are on conservation lists and must not be picked can give your sense of color and design a new lift. If you have ever been lucky enough to see a deep gully through which rushes a stream of turbulent clear water on a bed of mossy rocks between fern-hung banks, and sunshine filtered through the branches overhead, the rare and breath-taking sight of a Cardinal flower swaying gently with the water, with another in the shadow of the bank, and, if this were not enough, a little farther down a cluster of bright blue Forget-me-nots . . . this is a color scheme you will never forget, and will strive forever after to bring inside your house.

ELIZABETH BURRIS-MEYER

Hello . . . Please Come In!

A small bouquet in a Leeds china bowl on top of a very old sculptured open cupboard which displays other pieces of a Leeds china collection.

This entrance which leads into a great contemporary house makes a marvelous point: it is not necessary to stick to one period to achieve an effect. There are several pieces of Chinese art from various periods, old English furniture, Dutch pewter. The feeling upon entering is one of great beauty and yet not overwhelming because this is a warm and loving and welcoming house.

BOUNCING BET
Saponaria officinalis
Pink Family

Edging our roadsides and railroad tracks in midsummer, this charming plant was brought from England by the early settlers who used the lathering juice for laundering, which is why it is also called Soapwort. It is also called Boston Pink and Lady-at-the-Gate and has still more names. Color is white to deep pink. *Height: to 3 feet.*

The light pink of the bouquet of Bouncing Bet enhances the cream and wood tones of this entrance.

SILVERROD
Solidago bicolor
Sunflower Family

Belongs to one of the very difficult species of wildflowers with which even botanists have problems. This particular variety differs from its first cousin, the Goldenrod, because of its white (or silvery) flowers. It grows in dry woods from Canada south to North Carolina and west to Missouri. *Height: to 4 feet.*

New England Aster, please turn to page 14.

Goldenrod, please turn to page 50.

BITTER DOCK
Rumex crispus
Smartweed Family

A European weed which now lines our roadsides from summer through fall all over the United States. At first, green, flowers, stems, and leaves turn brown. The plant makes interesting shapes everywhere it grows. *Height: to 4 feet.*

A mixture of Silverrod and Goldenrod with New England Asters in a china bowl greets you as you turn the stairs in this traditional hall.

Small entrance hall of a prerevolutionary country house (note the beautiful hardware on the door) is enhanced by this bouquet of Bitter Dock in an old leather bucket which also serves as a doorstop.

BAYBERRY
Myrica pensylvanica
Sweet Gale Family

This shrub was known to the early settlers on our shores who made candles from the gray berries. Aromatic Bayberry candles are still made in New England in the Christmas season. The shrub has tiny white blossoms in April and May. Common in sandy or dry woodland soil and near coasts. Canada to Alabama. *Height: to 5 feet.*

BITTERSWEET, please turn to page 60.

NEW ENGLAND ASTER
Aster novae-angliae
Sunflower Family

This is one of the flowers which most brightens our autumn landscape, mixing its vibrant purple with the reddening and yellowing leaves. It grows along the roads and in the woods not only in New England but north to Canada and southwest to New Mexico. *Height: to 6 feet.*

This back entrance hall is decorated all year round with an early American pickle crock with fresh or dried Bayberry and Bittersweet.

New England Asters in an old pewter tankard in the entrance hall of a former farmhouse are charmingly reflected in the mirror behind them.

Spaces for Living

Living rooms, libraries, music rooms, dens, all look better and feel happier with bouquets of wildflowers in one or several colors regardless of time of year and whatever grows outside, in the fields and meadows, around the water and along the roads nearby.

VERVAIN
Verbena stricta
Vervain Family

This is a large, mostly American family with flowers blue, purple, pink, or white. Ours were bright blue. Vervain grows in the summer, in dry open places in New York, parts of Canada, Massachusetts, west to Montana, south to Tennessee and New Mexico, and West Virginia. *Height: to 4 feet.*

Blue Vervain is very exciting in this contemporary living room in a straight black pottery vase, which here stands on a marble-topped table by Saarinen.

CHICORY
Cichorium intybus
Sunflower Family

This plant was already known in early Egyptian times when it was part of the staple diet. It is still used in coffee and as a vegetable. One of its outstanding assets is the blue of its flowers; there is nothing quite like it in all of nature. It grows everywhere on roadsides, in fields and meadows from July to October. *Height: to 6 feet.*

EXTREME CLOSE-UP OF FLOWER

On a coffee table before a fireplace is a planter filled with ferns. (Although on the conservation list in New York, ferns may, of course, be used if they grow on your own property.) The bouquet in front of the unused fireplace is made of Chicory in a Swedish glass vase standing on the hearth. The blue of the Chicory was stunning against the white birch logs.

JOE-PYE-WEED
Eupatorium fistuloseum
Sunflower Family

Has many leaves in a circle; the flower heads form roundish clusters. The plant emits a pleasant odor. Grows in moist meadows, thickets, often near ponds and the like. Canada to Iowa, south to Florida and Texas. First purple, the flowers grow pink with age. *Height: to 9 feet.*

QUEEN ANNE'S LACE
Daucus Carota
Carrot Family

Pliny describes this truly queenly flower as growing in Crete. Later, in England, during Queen Anne's reign, someone thought the flower looked like the lacy headdress of the monarch and gave it its present name. When fully grown the flower has a tiny deep purple center. When the seeds form, the flower head bends inward, forming something that looks like a "bird's nest" —another one of its popular names. It grows all summer, everywhere. *Height: to 5 feet.*

Against the wall of the fieldstone fireplace shown in the last photograph, a close look at a stunning bouquet of Joe-Pye-Weed, Queen Anne's Lace, and Vervain in an Italian wine jug. The vibrant glitter of the granite adds fire and movement to the simple flowers.

BLACK SNAKEROOT
Cimicifuga racemosa
Buttercup Family

This is one of the most graceful plants in our woods during the summer months. The majestic stalks weave in the breeze and it is wonderful to watch as the tiny flowers grow and open from the bottom to the top. Alas, the beauty of the plant is balanced by its odor, which has given it its Latin as well as its other, common, name, Bugbane. It is also called Rattle-top because the ripe seeds rattle in the breeze. It received the name by which it is most widely known because the Indians treated snakebites with its roots. Massachusetts to Georgia, Tennessee, and Missouri. *Height: to 8 feet.*

Black Snakeroot, Queen Anne's Lace, and Meadow Rue are here combined in a large iron pot in front of an early American mantle with soft green paneling. The effect of the all-white bouquet against the background was extremely pleasing. This could have been a hundred years ago.

SUGAR MAPLE
Acer saccharum
Maple Family

One of the most common and most beloved trees of the East and Middle West, it grows not infrequently to a height of 120 feet. Its wood is much used in fine cabinet work and its sap is used in the manufacture of maple sugar.

On an Early American mantle with a colorful glass-fronted clock stands a Bennington ware pitcher with maple leaves. The brown and red of the leaves match the pitcher and plate and old wood.

Coffee Tables and Such

CALIFORNIA POPPY
Eschscholtzia californica
Poppy Family

Named in honor of the Russian traveler and naturalist Eschscholtz, this lovely bright yellow flower grows in abundance along the roads of Arizona and California. The seeds have been brought East and many people now cultivate them in their gardens. Blooms all summer long. *Height: to 2 feet.*

FLOWERING SPURGE
Euphorbia corollata
Spurge Family

This belongs to a large family of flowers which grow all over the world. They bloom from June to October in dry fields and woodlands. Massachusetts to Minnesota and Nebraska; south to Florida and Texas, surprising everyone that the tiny yellowish green flowers are really single florets. *Height: to 3 feet.*

Few things could be simpler yet lovelier than California Poppies in a small cut-glass pitcher on a small round coffee table.

A bunch of Spurge in a bean pot . . . what could be simpler and more appealing on another small round table somewhere in a living room!

GROUNDNUT (Wild Bean)
Apios americana
Bean Family

One of the native plants of our country. (Some people consider it a parasite because it twines itself around shrubs and small trees.) The brownish pink or purple flowers are lovely as they cluster on the stalk. It grows in moist woods and thickets in late summer from Canada to Minnesota and Colorado and south to Florida and Texas. Pick sparingly to preserve it. *Height: to 8 feet.*

EXTREME CLOSE-UP

Groundnut, also called Wild Bean, is difficult to confine in small places. Here it makes an amusing display, extending, as it were, in all directions, in the tall contemporary purple glass bud vase from Sweden which rests on a nest of small tables next to the couch.

WILD or FALSE INDIGO
Baptisia australis
Bean Family

A rare and spectacular plant which grows in early summer in thickets and woods. It is a perennial American herb, found in Vermont, New York, Pennsylvania, west to Nebraska, south to Georgia and Texas. *Height: to 5 feet.*

BLUE FLAG
Iris prismatica
Iris Family

This plant, which can easily be recognized by its narrow leaves, grows in May to June in wet ground from Canada to Georgia. Its Latin name stems from the fact that the pods resemble a three-sided prism. *Height: to 3 feet.*

Wild (or False) Indigo in an Early American blue glazed pitcher makes friends with you as you pass the small table on which it stands. Some of the species of this plant have produced indigo-like dye. It is a much-branched bushy plant and very beautiful, even in the most elegantly cultivated garden. The blue flowers should not be picked but only the seed pods for propagation. We found ours in a friend's garden and could not resist showing it to you even in an extremely simple bouquet.

Blue Flag or Iris seems to have been born for a contemporary bud vase such as this. The purplish dark blue of the flower and the dark purple of the vase complement each other in extraordinary fashion.

Side Tables

DAY LILY
Hemerocallis fulva
Lily Family

Early summer brings us the blaze of orange which edges our roads and woodlands, often as far as the eye can see. There are eight or nine blossoms on each plant with one or two open at the same time. This is one of the reasons Day Lilies are useful indoors. While one finishes blooming the next one opens up. Some people claim Day Lilies make a fine salad, raw or cooked. This, however, depends on your pioneering spirit in cookery. Day Lilies grow everywhere in the U.S. *Height: to 6 feet.*

Snakeroot, please turn to page 22.

We continue with side tables in our living rooms . . . and have here made a bouquet of the spectacular Day Lilies mixed with Black Snakeroot. The combination in an old wooden mortar should appeal to sophisticated tastes.

YELLOW FOXGLOVE
Digitalis ambigua
Figwort Family

Digitalis is a native of Europe and western Asia and has long had a name for itself as an effective medicine for heart disease. It now grows in our northeastern woods, from June to September. *Height: to 6 feet.*

BLUEBELL
Campanula rapunculoides
Bluebell Family

An immigrant from English gardens as early as the seventeenth century, this lovely plant blooms all over New England and into the Midwest at the sides of the roads and in thickets in July and August. Some writers call it *European Bellflower* to distinguish it from Scottish Harebell (Bluebell). *Height: to 3 feet.*

SWEET CLOVER (Sweet Lucerne)
Melilotus officinalis
Bean Family

The flowers of this clover are just like all other clover flowers but grow on slender spikes. Sweet Clover is bushy and weedy and grows almost everywhere, on roadsides, in fields, meadows, and waste places in the Northeast, in fact everywhere in North America. When crushed, the stems and leaves smell sweetly. It makes good pastures and its hay was in demand in England as early as the sixteenth century when the gentry endorsed it. *Height: to 5 feet.*

QUEEN ANNE'S LACE, please turn to page 20.

To fill an oval container such as this tin basket requires more skill than just using the usual round vase or bottle. Begun with the central flower, Queen Anne's Lace, the bouquet was gradually expanded, as it were, into the full size of the container. The light yellow of the wild Foxglove mixed well with the delicate blue of the Bluebells and the darker yellow of the Sweet Clover emphasized the delicacy of the other plants.

For Any Kind of Table . . . Among the Very First Decorations in Spring!

SPICEBUSH
Lindera benzoin
Laurel Family

The tiny golden yellow blossoms of this shrub are among the very earliest promises of spring. Often in late March or early April before the leaves appear they will guide you through otherwise barren woods. Damp woods from Maine through the northeastern woods, west to Michigan and Texas, south to Florida. *Height 7 to 15 feet.*

Spicebush, whose golden shimmer brightens the woods almost before anything appears, is here put very casually into a "battery jar." This got to be so light and ethereal-looking that several people who came by exclaimed: "Ah, a Japanese arrangement!" No comment.

SHADBUSH (Juneberry, Serviceberry)
Amelanchier canadensis
Rose Family

In boggy meadows, along the road, and in the woods Shadbush appears in a veil of snow-white blossoms from Maine and western New Hampshire, west to Iowa and Kansas, and south to Georgia and Louisiana. The name Juneberry is said to have been given the shrub because it has crimson fruit in June; and Serviceberry because Indians, after much pounding and crushing, made cakes from the berries. The wood can be used for tool handles, canes, and umbrella handles and sometimes fishing rods. *Height: to 30 feet.*

Another early flowering tree is Shadbush, which looked stunning in this white apothecary jar. When Shadbush appears we know that May is here—as though the fishermen among us didn't know, for now the shad are running. Also among us is the shadfly, a less delightful creature . . .

PUSSY WILLOW
Salix discolor
Willow Family

Widespread in the northern temperate zone. The fuzzy catkins we know so well soon turn into dainty yellow flowers. Grows in low wet lands, riverbanks. Long lasting indoors. *Height: to 20 feet.*

SLENDER WILLOW
Salix petiolaris
Willow Family

Grows in damp soil—this one we found at the edge of a swamp—and blooms a little later than the Pussy Willow, from Canada to Michigan and Wisconsin and south to Tennessee. The catkins have a lovely grass-green color. For one reason or another, this is an appealing plant. *Height: to 12 feet.*

Good old and familiar Pussy Willow too is a harbinger of warmer days. Here it is in a soup can (label removed) and accompanied by a turtle made of stones. This could go into a child's room, but there are still older people around who are not ashamed of playing. This combination, in actual fact, brightened for quite a while the life of a patient.

Another member of the very large Willow family is Slender Willow, well named for its beautiful configuration. It too blooms in the early days of spring. Here we put it in a dark green French truffle bottle. Good anywhere.

CANADA MAYFLOWER (False Lily of the Valley)
Maianthemum canadense
Lily Family

These fragrant flowers grow in the woods and in moist crevasses from Canada to Tennessee, May to July. *Height: to 7 inches.*

EXTREME CLOSE-UP

DANDELION
Taraxacum officinale
Sunflower Family

This often blooms from early spring to autumn and is one of the plants known all over the world. Nor does it lack true values. One writer states that the United States annually imports one hundred thousand pounds of dandelion roots for medicinal purposes. The flowers are used for making wine and the leaves for greens. There are more than a thousand species of the plant in the world. The name was contrived because the leaves resemble lions' teeth. *Length of leaves: to 10 inches.*

Canada Mayflower makes a carpet of white and green in the woods in spring. It is a small flower on a short stem and the white china match container in which it was photographed seemed the most fitting and perfect vase.

The marvelous golden Dandelion—a weed, it is true, but what a nice one—which carpets our fields and meadows before most other flowers, takes on something like elegance in this old English pewter tea caddy.

Arts and Flowers

BLUE VETCH
Vicia americana
Bean Family

A trailing or climbing plant found in fields, meadows and waste places, woodlands and along the shore. Often on the same raceme the colors vary from pink to purple. An émigré from Europe, vetch is now established from Canada through New England to Michigan. Blooms from June to August. *Length: to 3 feet.*

YELLOW CLOVER (Hop Clover)
Trifolium agrarium
Bean Family

As the Latin name implies, this species is "of the fields." For description of clover, please turn to page 162.

Although one does not usually buy art to hide it with flowers, sometimes flowers (or plants) enhance pictures; here we have tried. The well-known copy of Agamemnon's cup here stands before a photograph of the Acropolis and is filled with two flowers which one may find in Greece.

COMMON ST.-JOHN'S-WORT
Hypericum perforatum
St.-John's-Wort Family

Originating in Asia, this plant, which belongs to a very large family, now grows everywhere in the United States on roadsides and in waste places during the summer months. Its sunlike yellow sheen and its numerous flowers brighten any place it is brought to. *Height: to 2 feet.*

MEADOWSWEET (Queen of the Meadow)
Spiraea latifolia
Rose Family

The tiny white and pink flowers of this plant form a pyramidal design on successive stems, thus when fully open, a marvelous lacy show of fluff. It grows in wet meadows and rocky places from Canada to North Carolina, Missouri, and South Dakota. From June to August. It is a large herb. *Height: to 5 feet.*

Yellow and pink flowers in a black tole tea caddy enhance the mellow gold and black ikon of the Madonna of Częstochowa, the original of which is in an ancient Polish monastery and is thought to have been painted by St. Luke.

CAT-TAIL
Typha latifolia
Cat-tail Family

Grows in coastal waters, inland ponds, wet ditches, moist meadows, marshy ground all over North America. The flower, which is made of countless tiny florets, being brown, may not be the prettiest but there is something stately and dramatic about the long stalks. *Height: to 8 feet.*

NOTE: Grasses, not being flowers, have not been identified in this book, but they are highly recommended for use *with* other plants and they are, of course, everywhere.

This painting by Charles Burchfield, "Cobwebs in Autumn" (1948), made a perfect foil for the large bouquet of Cat-tail and grasses in the Dutch pewter pitcher before it. They are mutually flattering and even now, after several months, enhance the hall in which they preen themselves.

GOLDENROD
Solidago canadensis
Sunflower Family

There are said to be around seventy-five species of Goldenrod in the United States, their flowers all more or less alike, except for the way in which they grow. Some go out straight, others in swathes, some close to the stem, some in long racemes. The one in this picture is easily recognized for its growing habits. It appears from Canada to North Carolina, Tennessee, South Dakota, and New Mexico in late summer and autumn, on roadsides and in woodlands.

Solidago comes from the Latin *solidare*, to join or make whole. It has an ability to heal wounds. *Height: to 5 feet.*

This painting of a church in Nyack, New York, by Dorothy Deyrup is another example of how well art is served by nature. The large sunshine-yellow bouquet in front of it gives the painting another dimension.

Libraries

FIELD MUSTARD
Brassica campestris
Mustard Family

As with other plants, when Mustard is cultivated it is an important food. When it is wild, farmers call it a pest and a weed. There are a great many varieties growing all over our country from early summer often into autumn, in fields, roadsides, meadows. They were brought from the Old World. *Height: to 6 feet.*

A library is another place where wildflowers look their best. A big bunch of Mustard in an Early American ruby pitcher enhances the bindings and makes them look as though they too were part of the setting.

DOGBANE
Apocynum androsaemifolium
Dogbane Family

All through the summer and in nearly all of the United States this shrub which grows in thickets and fields sends forth its tiny light and deep pink striped flowers. One of Dogbane's other names is Indian Hemp. The fibrous bark was used by the Indians to make cords and cloth, and the roots were used for medicine. *Height: to 4 feet.*

This reach-through goes from a library into the kitchen and is handy for serving things across it. A grandmother's white china tureen with a gold and black design stands here filled with Dogbane, that delicate pink-flowered shrub whose blossoms smell as sweetly as they look.

SKUNK CABBAGE
Symplocarpus foetidus
Calla Family

The purplish brown spathe of this extraordinary plant—which grows in swampy places and generates so much heat in growing that often it peeks through the snow surrounding it—truly announces spring. The large leaves —sometimes three feet long—come later. All parts when broken have an unpleasant odor. From Canada south to Virginia, west to Ohio, Illinois, Iowa. *Height of the spathe: 4 to 8 inches.*

COLTSFOOT, please turn to page 84.

CELANDINE leaves are sturdier than the plant which has yellow blossoms, blooms all summer, and belongs to the poppy family. Does not last.

PICKEREL WEED
Pontederia cordata
Pickerel Weed Family

This is one of the most beautiful of aquatic plants. The deep blue of its flowers makes it stand out among its leaves, which are either heart- or lance-shaped. The part of the plant which shows above the water is usually one foot long. The rest grows in the hidden soil under the shallow water of the edges of lakes and ponds. It grows during the summer and autumn from Canada west to Minnesota, south to Florida and to Texas. It is indigenous to the United States.

EXTREME CLOSE-UP

Put the fruit of Skunk Cabbage, Celandine leaves, a couple of flat stones, and a single blossom of Coltsfoot into a black iron frying pan and you have an unusual bit of decoration on a small, modest library table.

On the other hand, Pickerel Weed is almost a harbinger of autumn! Here it was placed in a truly Art Nouveau silver vase which never looks out of place.

EXTREME CLOSE-UP

GIANT PURPLE LOOSESTRIFE
Lythrum salicaria
Loosestrife Family

Another one of the European imports that has established itself on our roadsides, in meadows, swamplands. It grows from June to September from Canada to Minnesota, south to Virginia and Missouri. *Height: to 3 feet.*

Pianos are fine places for decorating such as this one with the blue Mexican glass; it should help the practicing of scales if next to your music is that gorgeous flower which in August fills the meadows everywhere.

BITTERSWEET
Celastrus scandens
Staff Tree Family

This is a well-known climbing shrub common on old walls and in thickets, often climbing trees to a height of twenty feet. Its flowers, which bloom in June and are tiny, are rarely noticed, but come September they grow into beautiful orange berries forming bright clusters which will last all winter long, particularly if taken indoors before the berries open. Along roadsides and streams from Canada south to the mountains of North Carolina, to New Mexico.

An almost majestic showing of a great mass of Bittersweet in an antique Chinese vase standing on its traditional black lacquer base. The whole room vibrates with lights and shadows. Perhaps plants make their own music.

BLACK-EYED SUSAN
Rudbeckia serotina
Sunflower Family

This is a native American flower which grows during the hot summer days into early autumn, often making a sheet of deep yellow in a meadow, a true "summer carnival" in fields and along the roads. Some less lyrical souls call it a common weed. It got its name in honor of Dr. Olof Rudbeck, who taught botany in Sweden before Linnaeus. From Canada to Colorado, and to Florida and New Mexico. *Height: to 3 feet.*

Queen Anne's Lace, please turn to page 20.

Giant Purple Loosestrife, please turn to page 58.

At work too one needs cheering up. A designer or architect, in town or in the country having someone put a little bouquet so he can see it, will have a happier day. Not a bad idea for all slaves everywhere.

And how pleasant to have a few of the gayest flowers in creation in one's workshop . . . even if the "vase" is only a red-painted coffee can!

Eight Period Pieces

CROWN VETCH
Coronilla varia
Bean Family

An émigré of Europe, this appealing plant has established itself on many of our roadsides, in fields, meadows and waste places. Like most vetches it can easily be recognized by the large number of narrow segmented leaves growing from the stem. The flowers, pink with lavender touches, are gathered into an attractive head. It grows in the summer in the Northeast and south to South Dakota, Virginia, and Missouri. A creeping plant. *Length: to 2 feet.*

ETRUSCAN

The Etruscans have remained one of the great mysteries of history. Although we know something about their arts, their way of living, their wars, their religion, we are still not sure where they came from or how they spoke.

The earth colors they used have remained almost untouched in the stillness of their burial places. This bouquet follows one of the wall paintings in its colors, for Crown Vetch is almost exactly like the pink seen in the small book in front of the bouquet. The colors of the vase and background emphasize the marvelous black of the vase, a copy of an Etruscan masterpiece in the Metropolitan Museum of Art in New York City.

WILD YELLOW LILY (Meadow Lily)
Lilium canadense
Lily Family

This is an indigenous species. The Indians are said to have used the bulb for thickening soup. It is a stunning plant, its color shining like gold against the green of grasses and trees. It grows in the summer all along the northeastern states, west to Minnesota, south to Virginia and Alabama, in fields, on roadsides and in woodlands. *Height: to 5 feet.*

DEPTFORD PINK, please turn to page 144.

GIANT PURPLE LOOSESTRIFE, page 58.

OX-EYE DAISY, page 112.

MEADOW RUE, page 100.

MIDDLE AGES

In almost all parts of Europe the Middle Ages was a time of wars, of injustice and disease. But it was also an age of deep piety, of gallantry, and one of the greatest and most unforgettable periods of art, most of which was dedicated to God and much to the re-creation of the deeds of the manly arts. This has come down to us in the marvelous tapestries to be seen in the museums of the occidental world.

Our bouquet with a keynote of yellow attempts to re-create a moment of meditation. Against a background of carved oak and next to a Gothic figure of St. Joseph, a multicolor bouquet rests in a pewter goblet.

WILD ROSE
Rosa virginiana
Rose Family

Fossil specimens have been found in Montana and Oregon which indicate that the Rose is actually much older than man. Today, it is said, there are more than thirty thousand specimens. The wild varieties are easier to define. The ones in our picture originated in Virginia and now grow (and shine) along the Eastern Seaboard, west to Wisconsin, south to Georgia and Missouri, along country roads, fencerows, in hedgerows. The early settlers are said to have planted rosebushes as windbreakers. The hips (berries) were good food in those days. *Height: to 6 feet.*

EARLY AMERICAN

This term now seems to embrace a longer period of time than this country has actually existed. Here too we have an unhistorical if quite charming array of things: a spice cabinet, probably early nineteenth century, a much older inkwell, one of the famous Booz bottles, a Jenny Lind bottle, and a Sandwich bottle. With all this we have two Wild Roses which since time immemorial and in almost all parts of the world have signified love.

The Booz bottle ("Old Cabin Whiskey") is made of amethyst-colored glass, the Jenny Lind bottle has a bluish hue, the inkwell is dark green, and the Sandwich bottle the famous lush blue. (Author's collection.)

For Black-eyed Susan, please turn to page 62.

SHAKER

In the late eighteenth century the pious sect of the Shakers created, in their daily arts, a new style dedicated to usefulness and simplicity and thus great beauty. The memory of the Shakers is now preserved in several museums well worth visiting.

The pieces here shown are original Shaker ware: the box in which seeds were kept, the small baskets for berries and nuts, and the larger basket in which we show only a bouquet of Black-eyed Susans and wheat, in keeping with the simplicity of the Shaker tradition. The wooden candlestick completes the picture, its design, too, free of affectation.

Incidentally, a pickle jar holds the flowers in place inside the basket.

MALLOW (Musk Mallow)
Malva moschata
Mallow Family

An Old World flower, it now grows over here on roadsides and in waste places in summer and autumn. It often makes spectacular displays; sometimes one flower is two inches across. The color varies from white to pink to purple. It is found from Canada to Virginia and west to Nebraska. The leaves emit a delicious musky fragrance, hence the name of this species. *Height: to 2 feet.*

YARROW, please turn to page 101.

EMPIRE

This portrait of a great lady in her wedding dress painted in 1825 was chosen as the perfect background expressing everything the period of the Empire was: love of luxury, a sumptuous life, a great sense of color in decoration and the arts, a tradition of formality and grace.

The wedding dress, as you can see, was in the palest lavender. We were lucky to find the Mallow which matches it. Yarrow which accompanies it repeats the lacy effect of the gown. The container is a green cut-glass goblet from Bohemia made at about the time of the portrait.

VETCH, please turn to page 44.

MILKWEED
Asclepias syriaca
Milkweed Family

This extremely common but nevertheless quite beautiful weed was named in honor of the Greek physician Aesculapius. The species "syriaca" is thought to have originated in Syria. Its most outstanding feature is the construction of the blossoms, which makes the perfect insect trap. It has a milky juice to which some people are allergic, so be careful! Milkweed blooms in the summer in fields, prairies, on roadsides, from Canada to Georgia and Missouri and Nebraska. *Height: often as much as 5 feet.*

ART NOUVEAU

The lush and somewhat overwhelming period of art at the turn of our century called Art Nouveau is now again, for one reason or another, quite in vogue. Ten and twenty and thirty years ago we sneered at it; who wouldn't laugh at the Tiffany glass lampshades which used to decorate people's "salons" (now called living rooms). Still, the movement showed vigor and imagination, a riotous use of color and shape, and so now it is with us again.

We had a great deal of fun re-creating this piece of Art Nouveau: using an amethyst-colored crystal vase with a silver neck (an authentic piece) for trailing Vetch and Milkweed, a silver cigarette box in front of it and a stunning multicolor Paisley shawl (all authentic) in back of it. We pride ourselves on having once again brought forth a Tiffany shade.

Swamp Candle, please turn to page 154.

Fringed Loosestrife, please turn to page 154.

CONTEMPORARY

One of the best known and liked expressions of modern design, this Calder mobile plays the keynote in this photograph. Its vibrating elements of color set themselves off against the black background, at the same time emphasizing the gold of the Venetian vase which holds a bouquet of Swamp Candles and Fringed Loosestrife.

This is another and actually very simple example of how well and easily decorating with wildflowers can work, in any place, at any time.

CORALBERRY (Indian Currant)
Symphoricarpos orbiculatus
Honeysuckle Family

In the spring the tiny flowers of this handsome shrub are white and pink. In autumn the berries are first coral-red and then crimson-magenta. It is an indigenous shrub in New York, New Jersey, and Pennsylvania, west to the Dakotas, south to Georgia and Texas. It also grows on rocky slopes and the banks of the Delaware River. It is often cultivated in gardens, and makes a nice showing in lawns. *Height: to 7 feet.*

JAPANESE

Our friends across the Pacific have enriched many of our lives with their ancient arts of formal design with plants, in gardens, in houses. It has now become quite "the thing" to attempt Japanese effects. We must remember, however, that unless we study seriously we shall never be able truly to understand the meaning of Japanese design, most of which is based on the ceremony and ritual of a formalized culture of great age and beauty that is very often outside our own emotional experience.

We believe we have come as close as possible to a Japanese concept. The flat iron vase into which we have put a spray of Coralberry is centuries old; the brown bamboo mat upon which it rests is a traditional accessory.

Bed and Dressing Rooms

DOGBANE, please turn to page 54.

EXTREME CLOSE-UP

SWEET WHITE VIOLET
Viola blanda
Violet Family

A small very fragrant variety which grows close to the ground and often dots shady meadows or woodlands. It is veined and bearded. April to May from Canada to Arizona. Flowers are only a half inch across, so take care not to step on them!

FORGET-ME-NOT, please turn to page 96.

A breakfast or sickroom tray looks very much more cheerful with a small posy. Here are sprays of Dogbane in an old dark blue bottle.

White Violets and Forget-me-nots make a sweet little bouquet in this small urn with pedestal on a piece of Italian marble. Lovely on a chest!

STAR-OF-BETHLEHEM
Ornithogalum umbellatum
Lily Family

Grows sometimes along the road, often at the edge of woods. Bulbs are now sold in nurseries and plants have been acclimatized in gardens. Even a few plants make an enchanting display. Grows from Canada to Kansas in spring and early summer. *Height: to 12 inches.*

Star-of-Bethlehem, one of the most delicate and decorative wildflowers of the countryside looks just fine in this rather aged black bean pot.

SAXIFRAGE
Saxifraga virginiensis
Saxifrage Family

With its tiny white flowers in tight clusters and short leaves, this early spring plant grows in the small crevices of rocks or between rocks, and though you will have to look for it, you will be greatly rewarded when you find it. From Canada through New England hills and woodlands, west to Michigan and Minnesota, and south to Georgia and Tennessee. March to May. *Height: to 12 inches.*

EXTREME CLOSE-UP

COLTSFOOT
Tussilago farfara
Sunflower Family

Another flower of early spring, coltsfoot derives its name from the resemblance of its stem to a young horse's foot. Its bright yellow dots damp places and often roadsides from Canada to New Jersey and Minnesota. *Height: to 18 inches.*

Saxifrage, one of the early spring plants, extremely delicate and pretty, looks very decorative in these small old perfume bottles, whether it is barely open or in full bloom. In the small brown bottle in the shape of a little man, with a label describing a "Japanese Polish," are several Coltsfoot blossoms, all of them lovely on night tables.

EXTREME CLOSE-UP

BEARDTONGUE
Penstemon digitalis
Snapdragon Family

On woodlands, fields, and along many of the older roads are the graceful wands of this delicate and lovely plant. Sometimes tinged with purple, it is easily recognized by the shining flowers against the grass or undergrowth. Maine to Minnesota and Texas. An American perennial, late spring and early summer. *Height: to 5 feet.*

BLUEBELL, please turn to page 34.

Beardtongue in this tall barbershop bottle looks refreshingly spruced up. It is one of the most appetizing flowers in creation, indoors or out.

A pair of French bottles of the Victorian era here hold two tall bouquets which emphasize the shape of the containers. To the left is European Bellflower, to the right, Beardtongue.

CINQUEFOIL
Potentilla recta
Rose Family

Gets its name from the French for five leaves. Sometimes the blossoms are mistaken for wild Strawberry. Those of this species, however, are pale yellow. Cinquefoil grows along the roads and in waste places from May to August, in the Northeast and south to North Carolina, west to Minnesota. The *P. recta* comes from Europe. *Height: to 2½ feet.*

CONEFLOWER, please turn to page 158.

SWEET PEPPERBUSH (White Alder)
Clethra alnifolia
White Alder Family

Come August the air gets sweet because the Pepperbush is in bloom. The flowers themselves are tiny but there are a great many of them on the slender terminal clusters of the branches. In moist woods and wet soil, from Maine to Florida. *Height: to 10 feet.*

A bouquet near your toothbrush or soap dish may help the daily chores.

Children's Rooms

EXTREME CLOSE-UP

DANDELION, please turn to page 42.

CONFEDERATE VIOLET
Viola priceana
Violet Family

This is probably not a strictly wild violet, but it had escaped into the wilderness where we found it. In our area there are fifty-one species of violets, many hybridized so that their original characteristics are no longer pure. At any rate, they are lovely whatever their kind and place. All bloom in spring, in moist places from Canada to Minnesota, Nebraska and Arkansas. *Flowers are about ¾ inch.*

STAR THISTLE (Bachelor's Button)
Centaurea cyanus
Sunflower Family

This is the Cornflower of England and the Continent. It is much bluer there, more like our cultivated variety, which is pinkish purple. It blooms in late spring and through summer along the roads, in fields and waste places almost everywhere in the United States. *Height: to 2½ feet.*

Two young people actually made the bouquets on this page and were proud of them. The introduction of the model cars was quite deliberate.

BONESET
Eupatorium perfoliatum
Sunflower Family

Old-timers often used this herb for brewing bitter tea. Together with its purple brother, Joe-Pye-Weed, it grows in moist areas of meadows and roadsides. It comes to full ripeness in early fall and provides ample food for honeybees. It is also called Thoroughwort because the stems seem to grow through the leaves. Canada to Florida and Texas. *Height: to 5 feet.*

PICKEREL WEED, please turn to page 56.

HARDHACK (Steeplebush)
Spiraea tomentosa
Rose Family

The spire of small pink flowers makes a decorative addition to any bouquet and lasts especially well indoors. It has attractive woolly leaves. Hardhack grows in wet meadows or just well-drained soil from Nova Scotia to Arkansas. *Height: to 4 feet.*

Boneset, Hardhack, and Pickerel Weed in a brilliant blue glass pitcher look great on a marble topped kitchen table which is also for eating.

EXTREME CLOSE-UP

BUTTERCUP (Crowfoot)
Ranunculus bulbosus
Buttercup Family

One of the most familiar flowers of the fields and meadows, this belongs to an almost world-wide group of herbs. The Latin name *Ranunculus* (little frog) was given it by Pliny when he saw the aquatic species where small frogs abounded. *Height: to 1 foot.*

GOLDEN ALEXANDERS (Golden Meadow Parsnip)
Zizia aurea
Parsley Family

The first of the Parsley Family to appear in early spring, in open woodlands and sometimes near country roads, was named for J. B. Ziz, a Rhenish botanist of the late eighteenth century. It is a North American perennial whose tiny flower heads form widely separated clusters. From Canada to Texas. *Height: to 3 feet.*

WHITE CAMPION
Lychnis alba
Pink Family

This graceful yet sturdy white flower dots the fields and meadows from late spring to early autumn. It is related to the better known but smaller Bladder Campion; as it grows, its calyx too becomes enlarged. It is a weed that came to us from Europe. Its name comes from the Greek, *lychnos*, lamp. Campions grow in fields and on roadsides, almost everywhere in the United States. *Height: to 2 feet.*

HAWKWEED
Hieracium pratense
Sunflower Family

The common name of this bright yellow flower comes from Pliny's suggestion that hawks use it to better their eyesight. The orange variety named Devil's Paintbrush often grows side by side in the same meadow. Hawkweed came to us from Europe and now grows in the Northeast to Georgia and Tennessee. *Height: to 3 feet.*

Fill a blue Dedham-ware mug with buttercups and your kitchen will look as though a little sunshine had entered it. Good anywhere at all.

A giant decorated coffee cup makes a good container for a mixture of Golden Alexanders, Buttercups, Campions, and Hawkweed.

Flowering Spurge (Tramp's Spurge), please turn to page 26.

FORGET-ME-NOT
Myosotis scorpioides
Forget-me-not Family

In quiet waters and on wet ground grows the wild Forget-me-not which is deeper blue and longer lasting than its cultivated relative. It is one of the best known flowers anywhere and one of the most beloved. One writer says it is "the symbol of faithful love and undying memory." In Greek, *myosotis* is mouse ear. Grows all summer long. *Height: to 18 inches.*

Sweet Pepperbush, please turn to page 88.

Anywhere in your kitchen you will find room for this quite ordinary cup filled over the brim with Flowering Spurge and Forget-me-nots.

Sweet Pepperbush in this pewter pitcher may give you an idea how to have something nice-looking and sweet-smelling near your telephone when you must call your plumber, carpenter, oilman, electrician, local garage, or a friend.

DANDELION, please turn to page 42.

PHLOX

Phlox divaricata
Phlox Family (Polemoniums)

This delicate flower whose center is sometimes pink grows from April to June in rocky woodlands and open places. It is often called Wild Sweet William, which, as a prominent botanist says, "is misleading. Sweet William is in the Pink Family." Northeast to Middle West, south to South Carolina, Alabama, and Texas. *Height: to 3 feet.*

The humble Dandelion combined with the lovely lavender Phlox looks very appetizing in this hand-painted white teapot with its black handle.

MEADOW RUE
Thalictrum polygamum
Buttercup Family

This graceful white plant is one of the spring and summer flowers growing along the roads, in meadows and thickets, from Canada to Georgia and Indiana. It is lacy and fluffy. *Height: to 8 feet.*

BEARDTONGUE, please turn to page 86.

HEMLOCK PARSLEY
Conioselinum chinense
Parsley Family

Although its name is not inviting, it is perfectly harmless if you wish to eat it. But be careful, there *are* poisonous hemlocks which resemble it. It looks smashing in a bouquet and that is really enough for any plant. Summer, in most places of the Northeast and Midwest. *Height: to 5 feet.*

EXTREME CLOSE-UP

BEDSTRAW
Galium aparine
Bedstraw Family

Coming to us from England this delicate plant is a relative of coffee and its seeds are said to be a good coffee substitute. It has a way of clinging to one's clothes and to animals' fur, which may be one reason why it is found in so many places around the world. *Height: to 4 feet.*

In a small white and blue pitcher—in the much loved Meissen blue onion design—with a matching rolling pin in the background, this all-white bouquet is a perfect idea for a summer kitchen, pantry, or even laundry.

EXTREME CLOSE-UP

YARROW (Milfoil, Soldier's-Woundwort)
Achillea millefolium
Sunflower Family

This is a well-known weed in almost all the temperate zones of the world. The translation of the Latin name means something like "the thousand-leaf plant Achilles used." Perhaps it *was* the herb that Achilles used for healing wounds. Grows everywhere and anywhere. *Height: to 3 feet.*

FLEABANE
Erigeron annuus
Sunflower Family

Everywhere in the United States grows this tall plant with many small white flowers from late spring to early autumn, in waste places, fields and meadows, and on the roadsides. It is easily taken for its first cousin, Robin's Plantain, which has identical habits, but is lightly purple-tinged. *Height: to 5 feet.*

A white porcelain mortar—used in pharmacies and chemists' shops—with its pestle beside it, is here filled to the brim with Fleabane. This bouquet gave us great pleasure: so pretty and so little work!

Places for Dining

WATER LILY (Water Nymph)
Nymphaea odorata
Water Lily Family

Who has not stood at a pond full of Water Lilies floating gracefully among their leaves and letting you share their fragrance? Characteristically, their petals diminish in size and finally become stamen in the center of the flower. Probably a native of eastern Asia, it has come to us from Europe. It blooms in the summer and autumn. Don't pick it too freely. Many lakes and ponds have been "cleaned" and who knows how long this beautiful flower will be with us. From Canada to Florida and Texas. *Width of bloom: 3 to 5 inches.*

A formal, traditional, dinner table has here as its centerpiece a large silver dish whose removable insert, usually filled with fruit, now has a few white Water Lilies floating in the middle. The flowers will last for days. Don't worry if they close up at night. They do that even in the ponds in which they live, together with the rarer pink Water Lilies.
The rest of the table is set with family silver and china.

EXTREME CLOSE-UP

NEW YORK IRONWEED
Vernonia noveboracensis
Sunflower Family

A perennial herb which farmers dislike for the hardness of its stem and we love for the beauty of its deep purple flowers blooming in August and September when not too many flowers are left to bring inside. It grows in open woodlands and fields from Massachusetts to Georgia, Missouri and Ohio. *Height: to 9 feet.*

QUEEN ANNE'S LACE, please turn to page 20.

A formal, contemporary dinner table set with a Danish silver bowl, with three candle holders. The dazzling white contemporary pottery and even the Danish pewter and bone tableware are greatly enhanced by Queen Anne's Lace and New York Ironweed, which form the center decoration.

Centerpieces

BULL THISTLE
Cirsium vulgare
Sunflower Family

Thistles are generally disliked as pesky weeds, but some have beautiful flowers such as this one, which is easily recognized for its large head of "hair." But don't ever pick it with your bare hands; the stems are extremely prickly. The Bull Thistle grows throughout the United States, on roadsides, in fields, from summer to autumn. *Height: to 6 feet.*

GOLDENROD, please turn to page 50.

A very large dining table looks bare and even forbidding unless you put a bouquet in its middle. This one was made of Goldenrod and Bull Thistle, a stunning combination of autumn colors in a glass compote.

MOUNTAIN LAUREL (Calico Bush)
Kalmia latifolia
Heath Family

One of the most beautiful evergreen shrubs in our woods and hills and mountains with lovely clusters of pink flowers. In the South, it sometimes grows to thirty feet or more. It is named after the Swedish botanist Peter Kalm who visited here in the eighteenth century and sent plants to Linnaeus for description and identification. Actually the common name Laurel is a misnomer. The first settlers thought it looked like the Greek and Roman Laurel and therefore gave it that name. In our range it grows usually to 3 *to 6 feet.*

WHITE PINE
Pinus Strobus
Pine Family

Grows generally in light sandy soil from Canada to Ohio and along the Atlantic coast. It grows very fast and gives us hope that the terrible depletion of our forests will someday be remedied. The wood of this tree has from the days of the first settlers been most widely used for lumber and carpentry. *Height: to 50 feet.*

Branches of Mountain Laurel and White Pine make an impressive display in an early Wedgwood tureen, in the middle of a formal dinner or luncheon table, or, perhaps, a buffet, or chest of drawers in your dining room. The pink wheat design on the tureen matches the laurel.

OX-EYE DAISY
Chrysanthemum leucanthemum
Sunflower Family

This plant of Eurasian origin is one of the truly universally growing specimens of the world's flora. Here it is abundant from June to September along the roads, in open meadows, in waste places and even gardens. It has been a favorite of children and poets for a long time and in many places. It has also been the source for a number of home remedies—not necessarily recommended by the medical profession. *Chrysanthemum,* derived from the Greek, means "Golden Flower." It keeps exceedingly well indoors. It is said to be dedicated to St. John the Baptist. *Height: to 2 feet.*

The heads of Daisies floating upon the water in a contemporary glass bowl . . . what could be prettier, and easier, and more fun to do for your next small and intimate, but elegant dinner party?

APPLE
Malus sylvestris
Rose Family

Brought from Europe, the Apple now exists almost everywhere over here. An interesting fact is that it is most common along the waterways, which were the best means for distribution of seeds. Flowers in spring, comes into fruit in autumn. There are many varieties. The wood is hard and close-grained and often used for tool handles, because it is so tough. *Height: to 40 feet.*

Phlox Divaricata, please turn to page 98.

These Sandwich-glass flower holders—four are needed to make a circle —filled with Apple blossoms and *Phlox Divaricata* make a stunning display for the center of a dark wooden table, with or without settings.

BINDWEED (Wild Morning Glory)
Convolvulus sepium
Morning Glory Family

This beautiful plant with white, pinkish, or lavenderish flowers adorns the hedges and thickets everywhere in our countryside, and it is said that it grows into a complete circle in two hours twisting and twining around some shrub or fence. The flowers open completely in good weather, and by the light of the full moon. *Length: to 10 feet.*

SKULLCAP
Scutellaria lateriflora
Mint Family

The interest of Skullcaps lies in the remarkable design of the tiny individual flowers which make up the racemes—as the Latin name implies, which describes the projection like a bowl (*Scutella*) over the face of the flower. There are said to be over a hundred species in this country with minimal variations. The pink flowers of *S. lateriflora* grow everywhere in moist thickets and meadows during the summer and into autumn. *Height: to 2 feet.*

BUSH HONEYSUCKLE
Diervilla lonicera
Honeysuckle Family

A common North American shrub which was named after Dr. Dierville, who carried the plant from Canada to France as long ago as 1707. It grows from Canada west to Wisconsin and south to the Georgia mountains, and blooms in the summer thickets, dry woodlands, and, if you are not careful, all over your backyard. It has fragrant honey-colored flowers. *Height: to 4 feet.*

QUEEN ANNE'S LACE, please turn to page 20.

Bindweed, Skullcap, Bush Honeysuckle, and Queen Anne's Lace, counterclockwise, here fill the four crystal condiment bottles in a Victorian cruet stand, making an amusing centerpiece for any kind of party.

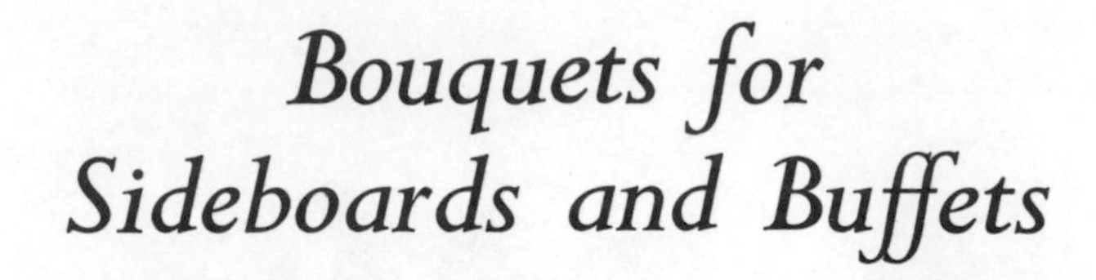

Bouquets for Sideboards and Buffets

Bitter Dock, please turn to page 12.

Sometimes just a board in front of a reachthrough from the kitchen will make a beautiful place for all sorts of buffets. The first photograph in this section was taken in a stunning contemporary house in which owner and architect made use of recessed illumination. This proved to be of particular interest in this bouquet of grasses and Bitter Dock where it brought into relief the simplicity of the material used. The bouquet stands in a brown Mexican earthenware bowl. It will dry out and then last for many months.

SWAMP MILKWEED (Cotton Weed)
Asclepias incarnata
Milkweed Family

The seeds of all this family have downy wings and, in addition, one of the most beautiful designs one can discover. In other ways this plant is useful: an extract of its juice is made to this day for asthma, dyspepsia, and cough. Blooms in summer, this particular species in wet and swampy places, from Canada to New Mexico. *Height: to 5 feet.*

MEADOWSWEET, please turn to page 46.

An oblong aluminum container with matching server (designed by the author) is here filled with an appealing mixture of Meadowsweet and Swamp Milkweed. The very light pink of the flowers from the shrub creates a pleasing play of colors with the pinkish purple of the weed.

Ox-eye Daisy, please turn to page 112.

Bitter Dock, please see page 12.

The two bouquets on these pages, made with Bitter Dock, illustrate how one plant (please also see pages 156–59) may be used in different ways. At the top are daisies with Dock in a cut vaseline-glass pitcher from Bohemia with two matching candlesticks; at the bottom left a Spanish basket with handle; but how different the two look! Setting, containers, background, all play an important part in the concepts of bouquets.

Porch and Verandah

WILD SUNFLOWER
Helianthus grosse-serratus
Sunflower Family

Although classed as a weed (so many of the most beautiful wild-flowers are) this deep yellow beauty does not act like one. Rather, it grows tall and sturdy and it is too large and lazy to get into pastures and fields. Yet cattle love it and get at it whenever they can. With "Helios" meaning sun, "anthus" flower, "grosse" large, and "serratus" rough, we have here the perfect descriptive botanical name. The plant grows in moist soil, along roadsides and in prairies. New York to Ohio, Arkansas, and Texas. *Height: to 10 feet.*

Screened- and glassed-in porches are perfect places for decoration with bouquets, for family or party moments. The first of these is built overlooking a lake and preparations are made for a buffet. On a bright red Indian sari is an orange tin plate with lemons and Wild Sunflowers. Tin plates and mugs in matching and contrasting colors with wood-handled tableware complete this extremely gay yet very simple setting.

Grass

Cat-tail, please turn to page 48.

Joe-Pye-Weed, please turn to page 20.

Boneset, please turn to page 92.

Behind the table on the previous page, in the middle of a serving cart, just then not in use, stands a straw ice bucket (with plastic waterproof insert) with a bouquet made of Cat-tails and grasses. How easy this was to do, and how effective! Of course, any ice bucket and any plant will do as long as it has the informality of outdoor living.

A very large window with a table in front of it acts just like a closed-in porch, bringing the outdoors inside. Here is a pewter bowl filled to overflowing with nothing more than Joe-Pye-Weed and Boneset, the same plant in two colors. They make the pewter glow.

BIRD'S-FOOT TREFOIL
Lotus corniculatus
Bean Family

A native of Europe—and no relative of the Egyptian lotus—it forms great sheets of luscious yellow along several of our new superhighways, ever occurring proof that nature, no matter what we may think, is stronger than man. From Canada to Minnesota, Virginia, and Ohio. It blooms in the summer. *Height: to 2 feet.*

If you wish to serve fish, this makes an amusing décor. Bird's-foot Trefoil is not a precious plant but it begins to look interesting coming out of a conch shell. A Japanese lacquer plate, a straw mat, and a shell make the perfect setting for a seafood luncheon, à deux or à quatre.

TURK'S-CAP LILY
Lilium superbum
Lily Family

A native American flower whose head seems to have reminded the early botanists who named it of a Turk's headdress. Each plant bears up to forty deep yellow or orange blossoms, a spectacular sight indeed along the road, in damp woods, or the edge of meadows, particularly when it has established itself and spread into big patches of shining and weaving color in the sunshine. Through New England, west to Minnesota, south to Georgia. *Height: to 8 feet.*

NOTE: Don't pick it wantonly. It needs protection.

Perched as it is here in an Early American glass bottle, high on a porch railing, the noble Turk's-cap Lily waves like a flag over the lake it surveys. Good idea . . . just be sure to secure the base of bottle to the railing with double scotch tape or a similar adhesive material.

WATER SMARTWEED (Redknees)
Polygonum coccineum
Smartweed Family

This grows on the shores of ponds and lakes, sometimes right in shallow and swampy water. Despite its brilliant rose color not many people notice it among the other weeds. Yet it looks wonderful in bouquets, particularly if its color is set off against grasses and leaves. Summer, throughout. *Height: to 3 feet.*

Meadowsweet, please turn to page 46.

Queen Anne's Lace, please turn to page 20.

Coneflower, please turn to page 158.

Floors too are suitable for bouquets if they are large and intriguing enough to fill the space well. Here is an assortment of grasses, Meadowsweet, Queen Anne's Lace, Water Smartweed, and Coneflowers. The container which is placed on a Japanese mat on a tile floor is a demijohn, a large glass vessel in which attar of roses is imported from Bulgaria. It was tricky to get that many stems through the narrow neck of the bottle but it worked and the outspreading stems repeat the movement of the plants on top.

Outdoors

MULLEIN (Peter's Staff, among many others)
Verbascum thapsus
Snapdragon Family

There are few more marvelous sights along a highway than a long row of Mullein in bloom. They stand like lighted candles with one or a few small yellow flames at any one time. For this is how the blossoms wander up the tall spike. Mullein flowers in late summer and autumn in fields, roadsides, and waste places everywhere in the United States. At one time Mullein was thought to be a remedy for leprosy. Thus the word Mullein, according to one writer, is a corruption of *mulandrum* from which was derived *melanders,* leprosy. A biennial. *Height: to 6 feet.*

Leaves of Mullein in the odd year.

Outside the house and all around it are usually more places for bouquets, even though you may have a cutting garden. The form and color of wildflowers are so different and often so dramatic that almost no garden flower can match them. Here are a few examples. First, a stately Mullein plant in a brown earthenware crock stands guard on the deck that leads into a contemporary house. Mullein is a biennial plant with beautiful leaves growing in the odd year. Here is a photograph of some of these.

VIPER'S BUGLOSS (Blueweed, Blue Devil)
Echium vulgare
Forget-me-not Family

This was brought from Europe and first established in Virginia from where it made its way north, south, and west so that now it can be found everywhere in this country. It loves sand and poor soil and the dustier the roadside along which it grows the more marvelous its pure blue and the dainty pink of the beginning flower (which is the reason for its having been put into the Forget-me-not Family with which it shares the color progression). *Echium* comes from the Latin and Greek words for "viper." The plant was considered an antidote against snakebites. "Bu-" derives from the Latin and Greek words for "ox," and "-gloss" from those meaning "tongue." It blooms in the summer. *Height: to 3 feet.*

STAGHORN SUMAC
Rhus typhina
Cashew Family

It is difficult to decide whether this is "Staghorn" or "Smooth" Sumac, they are so alike. Suffice it to say that this variety is not poisonous, and bears beautiful red berries in autumn. Cultivated in Europe, it grows over here in dry and gravelly soil from the Gaspé to Minnesota, Illinois, and Iowa. *Height: to 30 feet.*

Common Evening Primrose, please turn to page 142 for close-up and copy.

Giant Purple Loosestrife, please turn to page 58 for close-up and copy.

An old English brass fireplace bucket does itself proud on a porch with a huge bouquet in its hold, now that the fires are not yet burning.

Staghorn Sumac is characterized by red berries in early autumn. It is here shown in a low pottery bowl which stands in the center of a clockface drawn into cement within the brick floor of a large porch. Conceivably the bouquet or any one stationary branch could tell time.

Two Tables

BULL THISTLE, please turn to page 108.

NEW ENGLAND ASTER, please turn to page 14. (Here: close-up of flower head)

FLEABANE, please turn to page 102.

STAR THISTLE, please turn to page 90. (Here: extreme close-up)

As you sometimes relax with your paper on a late summer day, you may enjoy having close by a bouquet of two purplish pink flowers which blend together, and yet accent each other because they have such different shapes. Here a French tin mold holds the flowers and stands on a black metal table.

A very decorative idea in front of a corner of the house: this is a pottery vase from Arizona which looks grand on the Italian straw table.

COMMON MILKWEED, please see page 74 for whole plant.

Many people are unaware of the excitement given us in autumn by the seedpods of many plants which weave and glisten in the sun; often remarkable shapes almost mysterious in their strangeness. The Milkweed pods in a Turkish candy jar looked beautiful in their whiteness against the gray flagstone.

Special Occasions

COMMON EVENING PRIMROSE
(Night willow-herb)
Oenathera biennis
Evening Primrose Family

A very common and widely distributed weed whose beetlike roots have been used as foods and home remedies, probably by the Indians since this is an indigenous American plant. The flowers are bright yellow; they open in the evening and become fragrant as the night goes on. It is a biennial weed. Grows everywhere and blooms from midsummer into autumn, on roadsides, in waste places, fields. *Height: to 6 feet.*

Just leaves.

An outdoor picnic table is, of course, a natural for a wildflower bouquet. Take a Persian melon, hollow it out, put a jelly glass into it and fill it with Evening Primroses. Paper plates and napkins on a paper tablecloth, simple country tableware, and you have a gay and charming table.

Halloween, is, of course, the perfect time for informal bouquets. Here is a bunch of autumn leaves in a hollowed-out pumpkin. Couldn't be simpler.

BOUNCING BET, please turn to page 10.

DEPTFORD PINK
Dianthus armeria
Pink Family

A slender, delicate plant with long stem, long thin leaves, the whole topped with a tiny pink or rose flower of the most lovely design. Its bright color makes it visible in the grasses among which it grows in the summer, from Canada to Georgia and west to Missouri. *Height: to 2 feet.*

WILD BERGAMOT (Horsemint)
Monarda fistulosa
Mint Family

These shaggy and very appealing flowers come in pink, white, lavender, and purple and fill the summer air with their fragrance. Wild Bergamot is a member of an indigenous group of plants whose Latin name commemorates the French physician Nicolas Monardes who wrote about the medicinal value of many American plants. Both Indians and early settlers used *Monarda* for the cure or relief of several ailments. Bergamot's close relative, the bright red Bee Balm or Oswego Tea was much used by Indians for tea, and to cure colds. All grow in open woods, prairies, waste places, and all along country roads, almost everywhere. *Height: to 5 feet.*

QUEEN ANNE'S LACE, please turn to page 20.

BEARDTONGUE, please turn to page 86. (Here: another close-up view of the blossoms)

HEMLOCK PARSLEY, please turn to page 100.
MEADOW RUE, please turn to page 100.

For a simple outdoor tea party, put a big bunch of Bouncing Bet in a porcelain jug (this one is white and green Leeds). The light pink of one of our favorite flowers is accented by the much deeper pink, almost rose color of Deptford Pink mixed in with them.

For a cozy *Kaffeeklatsch* out of doors, put Wild Bergamot in a French milk can, use Austrian unbreakable pottery cups and an American aluminum coffee pot. This may not sound ultra stylish but the pinkish lavender of the flowers looked very chic on the red and white tablecloth. . . .

We could have decorated birthday cakes with daisies, or Christmas trees with apples. But we thought we would show you a bouquet which is not usually made of wildflowers: one for the bride. Of course it is an all-white bouquet and we have used everything in it in other bouquets. But this has a special pristine look as it is supported by a lace doily and held in a Paul Revere silver beaker.

How to Use Collections

Collecting coins or stamps or butterflies does not exactly suggest wildflower bouquets. Other collections do. We have tried to help you think how other collections *can* be combined with bouquets.

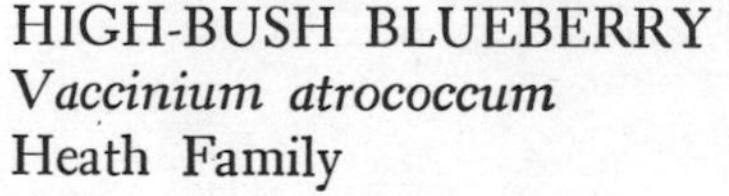

HIGH-BUSH BLUEBERRY
Vaccinium atrococcum
Heath Family

A favorite shrub of birds and children, it grows in meadows and thickets from Maine to Minnesota and south to Florida and Louisiana. *Height: to 15 feet.*

MOUNTAIN LAUREL, please turn to page 110.

SWAMP MILKWEED, please turn to page 120.

WILD IRIS (Blue Flag), please turn to page 30.

BOUNCING BET, please turn to page 10.

WILD SARSAPARILLA leaf, please turn to page 152 for plant description.

YARROW leaf, please turn to page 101 for plant description.

The first picture shows a collection of contemporary crystal fruit. Unseen in the center is a jelly glass with Wild Iris and Laurel blossoms. The effect was stunning on a luncheon table.

The second collection is one of antique crystal paperweights. In the middle are two triangular crystal ashtrays with Queen Anne's Lace and the leaves of a Wild Sarsaparilla plant. In another ashtray stands a branch of a High-bush Blueberry. Some of the paperweights were curved just enough at the top so that flower heads could be placed in them. On the left is Swamp Milkweed, on the right, Bouncing Bet. In a shell in the foreground (another collection) are several leaves from a Yarrow plant. The whole thing was unusual and interesting and created much comment at the cocktail party for which it was made.

Collections of old glass and bottles, of course, are the ideal things to use for wildflower bouquets. Here are a few of these.

Buttercup, please turn to page 94.

Golden Alexanders, please turn to page 94.

YELLOW GOATSBEARD
Tragopogon pratensis
Sunflower Family

The botanical name means "goat beard of the meadows"—another example of how colorful some of our botanical descriptions are. At any rate, this is a rather surprising flower growing from May to August almost everywhere in fields, on rocky banks and roadsides. The flowers close at noon and open up again at night. *Height: to 3 feet.*

WILD GERANIUM (Cranesbill)
Geranium maculatum
Geranium Family

The second common name was aptly given this flower for the formation of the long beak of the pistil. The plant whether in bloom or not is characterized by its much divided or cleft leaves. It is one of the great favorites in spring and early summer in open woodlands, fields, and sometimes waste places from Maine to Georgia, Arkansas and Kansas. *Height: to 2 and more feet.*

Yellow Goatsbeard, Golden Alexanders, and Buttercups make a symphony of yellow in an antique wineglass with gold design. (The foot of the glass broke and a black stand was made to hold it.)

This is a bouquet of Wild Yellow Foxglove and Wild Geranium in one of those Tyrolean bottles which Stiegel copied when he came over here in 1763. It has a colorful floral design in red, blue, yellow, and white which contrasted beautifully with the lavender and yellow of the bouquet.

WILD SARSAPARILLA
Aralia nudicaulis
Ginseng Family

The long horizontal roots of this plant are often used as a substitute for regular Sarsaparilla. It is characterized by the delicate lacy flowers which form a complete circle and grow two or more under an umbrella-like leaf which protects them from harm. It grows in woodlands from Canada down our Northeast to North Carolina and West Virginia, and west to Illinois, Ohio, Minnesota. It blooms from May to July. *Height: to 1 foot.*

Ox-eye Daisy, please turn to page 112.

Hemlock Parsley, please turn to page 100.

Buttercup, please turn to page 94.

White Campion, please turn to page 94.

In an American bottle with a fired design of the nineteenth century, we put one of our most beloved plants: Wild Sarsaparilla. Its beautiful lacy design seems to match the design of the bottle.

In this nineteenth-century dark green salt bottle we put a loose little nothing of a bouquet and it was charming.

FRINGED LOOSESTRIFE
Steironema ciliatum
Primrose Family

The "fringe" on this plant is on the base of the leaves; the flower, on the other hand, hangs its head toward the ground and you have to look twice to discover its pale yellow color and beautiful design. It grows during the summer in swamps, wet meadows, near brooks, almost everywhere. *Height: to 3 feet.*

SWAMP CANDLE
Lysimachia terrestris
Primrose Family

This plant is aptly named because, from the edge of a swamp or pond, you see these stunning flowers standing straight and proud, their yellow bright against the weeds and grasses. The close-up of the blossoms shows the delicacy of the design of the tiny flower. Grows during the summer in wet places from Canada to Georgia, Kentucky, Iowa. *Height: to 2 feet.*

Another collection which actually serves in several ways is displayed on one of the walls of a contemporary kitchen—proof once more that one does not need to be afraid to mix styles. The two Loosestrifes in the copper mold on the contemporary Lazy Susan are held in place by a small jelly glass in the middle of the mold.

One Flower

As we said before, it is a rewarding challenge to the imagination to try to discover in how many ways one can use *one* single solitary flower and still make it either a bouquet or something that serves a specific purpose or occasion. Of course, there is no limit to this kind of exercise. We are here presenting only two themes, in some variation.

BLUETS (Quaker-ladies, Innocence)
Houstonia caerulea
Bedstraw Family

A North American "original," light blue or white, covering many grassy meadows and places along the roads with sheets of heavenly color from April until June. Named for Dr. William Houston, 1695–1733, a Scottish botanist. Canada to Wisconsin, to Georgia, Alabama, Arkansas. *Height: to 8 inches.*

First, perhaps the loveliest of spring flowers in a very small perfume sample bottle.

And in a Bohemian cut Vaseline glass in which it cannot help but look as though it has considerably more elegance and stature.

GREEN-HEADED CONEFLOWER
Rudbeckia laciniata
Sunflower Family

The outstanding characteristic of this plant is that its petals hang down so that its center disk becomes almost the most prominent part. It starts greenish yellow and turns brown with age. It grows in moist thickets, around ponds and lakes from Canada to Florida and west to Colorado and Arizona, from July until September. *Height: to 9 feet.*

Second, an interesting-looking summer and autumn flower, which is shown four ways: on top in four bud vases as one might use them for place settings, at the bottom from left to right, in a Swedish Rose vase, in three small pottery vases, and in one of those ceramic insulators which the telephone company uses for its poles and sometimes forgets to take away.

Just for Fun!

And now that we have created all these unforgettable works of art, let us see whether we can't just play. For even in fun you can't go wrong with wildflowers, and hard as you may try you will not be able to make something disagreeable out of them.

FALSE SOLOMON'S-SEAL (Wild Spikenard)
Smilacina racemosa
Lily Family

This spray has creamy white flowers that turn into glassy red or purple berries in autumn. Country folk call it a plume. Grows in northern temperate climates, here from Canada to Georgia, west to Missouri, Arkansas, and Arizona, from May to July. *Height: to 3 feet.*

Someone had the bright idea to elongate a soft drink bottle. So we put into it a spray of False Solomon's-Seal.

WHITE CLOVER
Trifolium repens
Bean Family

This variety is only a small part of the enormous clover family, which is supposed to have three hundred varieties growing all over the world with only four native in this country. The Latin name *Trifolium* derives from "*tres*," three, and "*folium*," leaf. The plant is everywhere used for fodder but it also graces the fields and meadows of the temperate zones with the sweetness of its fragrance. Clover comes in many colors, red, pink, pink and white, yellow. The three-part leaf represented the Holy Trinity to the Irish. The doctrine of the Trinity was explained to them, so the tale goes, by St. Patrick with the help of the clover leaf. *Height: to 1 foot.*

Here we have one of those nineteenth-century labels which says: Crown dressing for Ladies and Children, Boots and Shoes, etc, etc. But the dark green bottle looked nice with a bunch of White Clover.

BUTTER-AND-EGGS
Linaria vulgaris
Snapdragon Family

It is easy to understand the common name of this flower; it has indeed the colors of two of our most common foods. In the olden days the juice of the plant mixed with milk was considered a fly poison, and even a beneficial skin lotion (depending, no doubt, on who tells what). Grows everywhere in waste places, on roadsides, even in gardens, all summer long. *Height: to 3 feet.*

FRINGED LOOSESTRIFE, please turn to page 154.

SWAMP CANDLE, please turn to page 154.

BLUE VETCH, please turn to page 44.

A chessboard is always decorative and while there is no game, why not decorate it a little more with a small white porcelain vase holding Butter-and-Eggs.

On the other hand, Blue Vetch always looks disorderly even as it cascades down the sides of this nineteenth-century green glass candlestick. Imagine candles big enough to fit a space in which flowers now rest in water. No wonder, they were plumber's candles!

Chemical glassware is among the most beautiful in existence, just as a plane or a bridge is beautiful for its total dedication to purpose and absence of curlicues and superfluous ornamentation.

We have here two variations: on top a "bulb" held by an ancient stand filled with Wild Sunflowers (see page 124) and Common Milkweed (see page 74). And at bottom in one of those most incredible glass creations called "three-neck, angle-type distilling flask," which gives us *three* chances for bouquets in one and the same container. We have used New England Aster (page 14), Joe-Pye-Weed (page 20), and Meadowsweet (page 46), and it all looked grand!

And now that you have read so much, seen so much, and learned so much, you can try to solve the picture on the next page.

What are the flowers we used? Do you know their color, their name, their time of blooming, their location, their use, if any, and your preference in your own house?

Well, at least have fun playing a new game.

How to Make Bouquets

There are directions and rules for making flower *arrangements,* as garden clubs and florists make them, but none for having fun with wildflowers. We, who wish to follow only our own inclinations and please ourselves and those around us, must learn to develop our own sense of shape, of color, of design. Certainly, all flowers can express a mood, a taste, a point of view, and they can fit well or not so well into a given space. It is questionable that you would put an enormous bouquet into a very small room, or some scrawny little thing in the middle of a large dinner table. But whether you use Black-eyed Susans or Daisies makes a difference only in color, not in scale.

Simply select whatever container will have the best size (and style) for a desired use, a given bunch of flowers, but remember one can make a very tall bouquet in a very shallow bowl or plate. This is where the few things come in you should know about for the mechanical ease of making bouquets. Plasticine, for instance, is a wonderful material for holding stout stems in whatever direction you wish to point them. "Pin holders," which come in many different sizes, are available in flower shops and most hardware stores; they too hold up flowers. Rings made of cork called "Flower Floaters" will hold one or several buds or flower heads on top of the water, let them float and prevent tipping over. We have used jelly glasses, frozen fruit and soup cans, low hors d'oeuvres jars and the like in many of our bouquets when we needed something to prevent a bouquet from falling inside a large container. There is also Styrofoam, which will hold almost anything, anywhere, in any way. The simplest of all to use are small pieces of hemlock or pine bows which will support anything the way one may wish. Nor must we forget lumps of wet newspaper which can be stuffed unseen around and between stems to hold them up. If you live in town and bring home a bunch of wildflowers to remember your fresh-air-and-sunshine weekend, your florist around the corner can probably help you.

Never *rip* a flower out of the ground; you will destroy the whole plant if you do. Always cut with a scissor or knife. Some flowers will collapse before you get them home; stick them into water immediately and they will revive. Better still, never go driving in the countryside without a bucket of water in your car. Study the habits of plants and remember that some last longer than others when cut and some not at all; some close at noon, some in the evening, and some open at night. Sometimes the plants are in shock when you bring them home and they have wilted; putting them in warm (not hot!) water for a while or giving them a couple of aspirins might bring them back to full glory. Above all, remember one thing: wildflowers are shy and simple things . . . don't fuss over them too much.

On Conservation

There exists a great deal of concern about the constantly disappearing natural treasures in forest, on mountains, in waters all over the nation. As more and more people expand, build longer and wider roads, more houses, establish more communities or expand existing ones, more and more trees are destroyed and not replaced; plants are wantonly hacked up and not transplanted, animals are left without food and die. Gradually the whole balance of nature is endangered; no scientific exploit will ever be able to replace the fragrance of a White Clover field or the color of Milkweed shining in early autumn in the setting sun. This is what conservation is all about: to protect from wanton and unnecessary destruction as much of nature as we can and to help build rather than destroy. In many instances we should have asked long ago, "Is this road necessary?"

Every state and every region in the country has laws to preserve certain plants, which may not be picked at all, or some only sparingly. But like everything, laws and conservation lists change and your local Garden Club will probably be able to inform you. Right now, for example, Ferns must *not* be picked anywhere in New York State because flower shops and butchers began to denude the woods of ferns to stick them into flower arrangements or use them as beds for meats. In Connecticut, however—our town is less than two miles from the border—we can still buy our steaks and chickens from trays bedecked with ferns.

By and large, a good and simple rule of thumb is not to pick any flower which propagates from seeds. It is usually safe to pick flowers which renew themselves from their roots.

Exempt from these rules are, of course the "weeds" such as Queen Anne's Lace, Buttercups, Daisies, Chicory, etc., which often make the most stunning bouquets and have renewed themselves unharmed year after year for many centuries past.

Do not *ever* pick any of the marvelous and rare flowers of the woods: Lady's Slippers, Orchids, Hepatica, Pitcher plants, Gentians, Cardinal Flowers, Pipsissewa, and so on. You may pick, say, Wild Sarsaparilla, Ginseng, and, of course, Evergreens, but that is about all.

Don't rip, *cut*. Don't leave ragged edges on stems or torn bark. Step carefully so that you don't destroy other plants around the one you want, even in a field or meadow. Don't pick from roadsides, let others enjoy them. And don't pick *all* the flowers from one plant. Leave enough for the next lover of wildflowers, and next year. You will leave a better-looking and healthier countryside behind you. The road to progress is surely not paved with the uprooted treasures of our land.

Some Good Books for Learning About Wildflowers

Botanists differ with one another just as other people do. Therefore one has to decide whose classifications to follow. The basic book, of course, is Asa Gray's *Manual of Botany*, 8th edition, American Book Co., New York, 1950, but it is too heavy and scientific for most people.

We have used Harold William Rickett's *New Field Book of American Wild Flowers*, G. P. Putnam's Sons, New York, 1963, as well as Edgar T. Wherry's *Wild Flower Guide*, Doubleday and Co., Garden City, N.Y., 1948, for basic identification.

But Ethel Hinckley Hausman's *Beginner's Guide to Wild Flowers*, G. P. Putnam's Sons, New York, 1948, is arranged by color and is by far the best book for immediate identification, even though some of the classifications have since changed.

An old favorite is Mrs. William Starr Dana's *How to Know the Wildflowers*, Charles Scribner's Sons, New York, 1924, which has recently been reprinted (1963) by Dover Publications, New York.

H. S. Zim and A. C. Martin, *Flowers*, Simon and Schuster, New York, 1950, is an inexpensive guide, also arranged by color and therefore useful, but not complete.

Another very special favorite is Edwin Rollin Spencer's *Just Weeds*, Charles Scribner's Sons, New York, 1957, in which all flowers that are known as weeds are described with enormous knowledge but also marvelously good humor. We have referred to it frequently for this book.

You might also try to find Homer D. House's *Wild Flowers of New York*, published by the New York State Museum, Albany, 1918. Some of the botanical data is different now, but the photographs are wonderful and most revealing. Many libraries have it.

Other good books are: R. S. Lemmon and C. C. Johnson, *Wildflowers of North America*, Doubleday and Co., Garden City, N.Y., 1961; F. A. Novák, *The Pictorial Encyclopedia of Plants and Flowers*, Crown Publishers, New York, 1966.

For trees and shrubs we used F. Schuyler Mathews' *Field Book of American Trees and Shrubs*, G. P. Putnam's Sons, New York, 1915, and George A. Petrides' *A Field Guide to Trees and Shrubs*, Houghton Mifflin Company, Boston, 1958.

Those of you who would like to know about wildflowers that can be grown in your own gardens, read *The Concise Encyclopedia of Favorite Wild Flowers* by Marjorie J. Dietz, Doubleday and Co., Garden City, N.Y., 1965.

And if you wish to continue studying nature at large, go to your library and read everything by Rutherford Platt, Hal Borland's *Sundial of the Seasons* which is a compilation of his nature editorials in the New York *Times* (J. B. Lippincott Co., Philadelphia, 1964), and everything by Jean Hersey and her *Guide to Wildflowers of the Roadside* (*Woman's Day* Magazine, New York, 1965) with photographs in color by the author of *this* book.

Index